# NEGOTIATING A BOOK CONTRACT

## A Guide for Authors, Agents and Lawyers

# NEGOTIATING
# A BOOK
# CONTRACT

## A Guide for Authors, Agents and Lawyers

Mark L. Levine

MOYER BELL | Wakefield, Rhode Island & London

Published by Moyer Bell
This Edition 1994

This book is designed to provide accurate and authoratative
information in regard to the subject matter covered. It is sold with
the understanding that the publisher is not engaged in rendering
legal, accounting or other professional services. If legal advice
or other expert assistance is required, the services of an attorney
or other competent professional person should be sought. While
every attempt has been made to provide accurate information,
neither the author nor the publisher can be held accountable for
any error or ommission.

**LIBRARY OF CONGRESS
CATALOGING-IN-PUBLICATION DATA**

Levine, Mark L.
    Negotiating a book contract.

        1. Authors and publishers—United States.
        2. Copyright—United States. I. Title.
    KF3084.L48    1988                          88-1436
    346.7304'82                                     CIP
    ISBN 0-918825-69-5 (pbk.)        347.306482

Printed in the United States of America
Distributed in North America by Publishers Group West, P.O. Box
8843, Emeryville, CA 94662, 800-788-3123 (in California 510-
658-3453), and in Europe by Gazelle Book Services Ltd., Falcon
House, Queen Square, Lancaster LA1 1RN England.

# CONTENTS

| | |
|---|---|
| Introduction | 1 |
| Grant of Rights | 3 |
| The Manuscript | 7 |
| Time of Delivery | 7 |
| What to Deliver | 7 |
| Satisfactory Manuscript | 11 |
| Return of Advance | 11 |
| Editor's Response | 12 |
| Indexes | 13 |
| Representations and Warranties | 14 |
| Indemnification | 16 |
| Relationship with Other Contracts | 19 |
| Publication | 20 |
| Changes in Manuscript | 20 |
| Title Approval | 20 |
| Cover Consultation or Approval | 21 |
| Copyright Notice | 21 |
| Copyright—"Work for Hire" | 22 |
| Advance | 23 |
| Amount | 23 |
| Timing | 25 |
| Bonuses | 25 |
| Flow-through | 26 |
| Miscellaneous | 26 |
| Royalties | 28 |
| "Standard" Royalty Rates | 29 |
| Hardcover | 29 |
| Trade Paperback | 30 |
| Mass Market Paperbacks | 30 |
| Children's Hardcover Books | 30 |
| Children's Paperback Books | 30 |
| Textbooks | 31 |
| Net, Royalties Based On | 31 |
| "Deep Discount" | 33 |

Other Reduced Royalties                           37
  Small Printings                       37
  Reprints                              38
  Mail Order                            38
Subsidiary Rights                                 39
  Introduction; List of Rights          39
  Points to Watch Out For—General       40
  Income                                43
    Division with Publisher   43
    When Paid (Flow-through)   44
  More About Certain Rights             45
Royalty Statements                                47
Termination                                       49
Out of Print                                      50
Effect of Termination                             52
Option                                            54
Competitive Books                                 57
"Next Book" Clauses                               59
Revised Editions                                  60
Other Important Clauses                           63
  Advertising and Material by Others    63
  Reservation of Rights                 63
  Affiliates                            63
  Arbitration                           64
  Assignment                            64
  Right to Audit                        64
  Credit                                64
  Return of Manuscript and Art          65
  Free Copies                           65
  Governing Law                         65
  Paperback                             66
Appendix—Sample Letter of Comments                67
Notes                                             79
Index                                             85

# INTRODUCTION

Most publishing contracts are written by publishers' lawyers properly looking out for the publishers' interests. It is my belief, however, that publishing contracts can readily be negotiated that balance the rights and interests—and meet the needs—of author and publisher alike. This book is designed to alert authors, and their agents and lawyers, to the many points that are either omitted entirely from some publishers' contracts or are written primarily from the publisher's perspective.

Authors should be aware that virtually every publisher regularly revises its standard contract in many areas when asked to do so by authors or their representatives. It is only the author who doesn't know that it is perfectly acceptable to ask for changes who signs the standard contract. Most of the points noted in this book can be obtained simply by asking; others may require harder negotiation.

Section headings in this book, as much as possible, have been designed to match the major sections and topics in a typical contract. This will enable the reader to compare his or her contract, topic by topic, with the comments in this book.

The sections in the book on grant of rights (items 4–6), "standard" royalty rates, advances and division of proceeds from subsidiary rights licenses apply both when a deal is being initially negotiated before any contract is sent, as well as

1

after the overall financial terms have been agreed upon and the publisher sends you its proposed contract. The other sections discuss topics that are generally negotiated only after you receive the proposed contract.

Please note that the points in this book are applicable whether the book is fiction or nonfiction, hardcover or paperback, for adults or for children, a textbook or for a general audience. They also apply regardless of whether one is negotiating with a major publisher, a university press or a small press.

References in this book to "authors" are generally also applicable to illustrators of children's books. For ease of reading, however, we use only the one term.

Paragraphs marked • or ○ are of especial importance (with those marked • being of greater importance).

Comments to a publisher can be conveyed orally or in writing. In general, it is best to list them in a letter that your editor can forward to the contracts department. A sample letter is in the Appendix on page 67.

In the past, many of the points mentioned in this book were handled informally between editor and author rather than included in the publishing contract. Because of the frequency with which editors now change jobs and the increasing changes in ownership of publishing companies, however, this fine and informal tradition can unfortunately no longer be relied on.

# GRANT OF RIGHTS

• 1.\* Be certain that you understand each right that the contract says you are granting (i.e., licensing) to the publisher. If you don't understand what a term means, ask. You may be giving something away unintentionally.

• 2. Be particularly aware of anything that says you are granting "all rights." This is not desirable. The phrase is too broad and could include all rights to the characters you have developed, related trademarks, your right to publish sequels and additional books in the same series, merchandising rights, performing rights, as well as certain traditional rights which should not be granted unwittingly.[1] It is far better to specify exactly what rights the author is granting to the publisher.

• 3. Be particularly careful about signing any contract that says you are writing the book on a "work for hire" basis or that categorizes you as an employee. This is not a standard publishing arrangement for book authors and should only be accepted with a complete understanding of the consequences. See "Copyright—Work for Hire" on page 22.

4. For each right granted, there are four factors to consider in the grant of rights section:

---

\*Paragraphs marked • or ○ are particularly important to an author (with those marked • being of greater importance).

The geographical area of grant.

The time period of grant.

The language of grant.

Whether the grant is exclusive or nonexclusive.

One or more of these is often missing from many standard contracts; it should be added if not there.

5. A publisher validly needs the exclusive right to publish the manuscript, in book form, in hardcover and paperback, in the English language, in the United States and its possessions, for a specified period of time (subject to an out of print clause), and the right to license reprint rights for such editions to others.

Anything beyond this is gravy to the publisher although the following rights are typically (and properly) also given under ordinary circumstances:

a. The exclusive English-language book rights for Puerto Rico and the Philippines. This is not objectionable.

b. The exclusive English-language book rights for Canada (though there is the start of a trend now to try to license these rights separately to Canadian publishers if the opportunity is there).

c. The *nonexclusive* English-language book rights for publication of the book throughout the rest of the world except for England, Ireland, South Africa, Australia, New Zealand (and possibly Canada).[2]

6. The rights for England, Ireland, South Africa, Australia and New Zealand are valuable and should not be lightly included. Authors represented by agents typically do not license these rights to the United States publisher but have their agent seek to license these rights abroad, directly or through subagents; exceptions are made here only when

the U.S. publisher's advance to the author is substantially increased to reflect the value of these additional rights.

Authors without agents or publishing contacts abroad should not mind licensing these rights to the U.S. publisher for a limited period of time provided that the U.S. publisher's share of any Commonwealth or other foreign licenses is not more than an author's agent and subagent would get. See "Subsidiary Rights—Income—Division with Publisher" on page 43 below.

○ 7. When licensing rights that are typically handled by an author's agent if he or she has one (performance rights, first serial rights, translations, and British Commonwealth rights) instead of being granted to the publisher, ask for a provision that requires each of those rights that has not been licensed after $x^*$ years from the date of the book's initial publication to revert to the author at that time. This will give you a second chance to license rights that the publisher has been unable to sell or has given up on.

8. Be aware that certain rights are implicitly granted under the typical grant of book rights unless you withhold them, so consider whether there are any areas or markets you want to withhold. Some examples of markets that will be considered granted under a typical contract unless withheld are premiums, large print, textbooks, specialty stores and book clubs.[3]

9. Where the grant specifies that the publisher may publish the book "in whole or in part," it is preferable to replace it with "in whole but not in part." If the publisher intends to publish one book as three separate books, you should know about that when negotiating your advance.

---

*Throughout this book, "$x$" is used as a number to be negotiated between the author and the publisher when the significance of the comment is not the specific number but the overall point made.

10. The time period virtually always specified for the publisher's exercise of the rights granted to it is the full term of the author's U.S. copyright in the work.[4] If the contract has a proper "out of print" clause (see page 50), this is fair for the basic rights granted.

11. Delete the word "sell" if it is used instead of, or in addition to, "grant" or "license." An author does not *sell* (i.e., permanently dispose of) his or her rights. He or she merely "licenses" them, i.e. "grants" the publisher the right to use them for a limited period of time in accordance with the terms of the contract.

12. Cautious authors will also clarify that the publisher's right to "license rights to others" does not apply to the initial publication of the book, which is the responsibility of the publisher you are signing the contract with.

13. For a further discussion of other rights requested and sometimes licensed to publishers, see "Subsidiary Rights" beginning on page 39. Some publishers include certain of these subsidiary rights in the grant of rights section; this is okay so long as the royalties payable if the publisher exercises these rights itself (and the percentage splits payable if they license them to others) are specified somewhere in the contract.

# THE MANUSCRIPT

## Time of Delivery

○     1. The contract will specify a date on which the manuscript must be delivered and say that if you do not deliver it on time, the publisher can cancel the contract. Ask the publisher to add a sentence stating that if the publisher wants to cancel the contract because the manuscript is late, it must first notify you in writing that unless you deliver the manuscript within $x$ days (30 or 60 days) from the date of that notice, it will then cancel the contract.

    2. Phrases like "time is of the essence" should be deleted. They mean that if you hand in the manuscript even one day late, the publisher can terminate the contract.

## What to Deliver

•     1. Specify everything. Avoid general phrases like "and all other materials. . . ." or "together with all maps, charts, illustrations, photographs, indexes and other materials which publisher deems necessary to the completion of the work." If you do not plan to deliver an item, cross it out. If you do, specify what kind, how many and the other data indicated below.

o    2. Describe the manuscript as accurately as possible to provide some objective criteria to help in determining whether the manuscript, when delivered, will be considered satisfactory. Possible ways are to specify:

Number of words the manuscript is expected to contain.

Number of double-spaced manuscript pages.

Number of black and white illustrations.

Number of color illustrations.

Nature and topic of book.

Fiction or nonfiction?

Audience the book is aimed at.

> For example, is it written for children, parents, scholars, lay persons, professionals, etc.? If for children, what age group? If a serious topic, will it be a scholarly treatment or a popularized one?

o    3. If photographs, charts, indexes, maps, illustrations, etc., are to be delivered, specify:

Which.

What kind.

How many.

Approximate size.

"Camera ready" or not.

> i.e., whether it is the author's or the publisher's responsibility to put them in a "form suitable for immediate reproduction" and who will pay for that. Preparing charts and other artwork in camera ready form should be the publisher's responsibility and be done at the publisher's expense.

In black and white or color (for photographs, maps and illustrations).

> If in color, will the publisher do the separa-

tions or is the author (or the illustrator, if a children's book) required to deliver black and white drawings with three overlays?

Also specify:
Who is responsible for getting them.
Who pays for them.
See point 7 below.
If full color drawings are being delivered, it is sometimes helpful to specify that the publisher will pay the separation costs.
Who makes the final decision on which go in.
Who has rights to them.

For illustrations and other drawings, you can even attach a sample of one of your drawings to the contract as an example of the illustrations' style. Just say that the style of the illustrations will be "substantially in the form attached." This can help against a second editor saying, after the fact, "The style just isn't what I'm looking for."

4. If the book will contain anything that the publisher is required to provide, that should be specified in the contract also.

5. On children's book contracts, clarify whether it is the author's or the publisher's responsibility to provide the artwork for the cover and book jacket.

Will there be a separate fee if the author/illustrator provides the artwork?

Or will they use one of the interior illustrations?

See above comments about color or not, separations, etc.

6. If the book is the type which will require a great many permissions from other copyright holders, ask the publisher to split the cost with you.

9

o    7. Although many standard contracts provide that the author is responsible for paying for indexes, copyright permissions, charts, illustrations, photographs and other visual material from his or her own funds, there are several alternatives that should be explored.

   a. Publisher pays the full cost of obtaining them and doesn't deduct the cost from future royalties.

   b. Publisher pays the full cost for them initially, but deducts it later from future royalty payments.

   c. Publisher pays the full cost initially, but deducts half of the cost from future royalty payments.

   If done this way or as described in point b. above, clarify that the author is not required to repay the publisher if the book fails to earn enough in royalties to cover the amount paid by the publisher on the author's behalf.

   d. Author and publisher split the initial cost, but publisher recaptures its half from future royalty payments to the author.

   e. Author and publisher split the cost, but the publisher is not entitled to get back what it pays from future royalties.

   The alternatives in c. and e. are generally considered fair to both parties and frequently given. There are good arguments for alternative a. however, especially for lengthy indexes, illustrations and other ancillary matter which can properly be considered the publisher's responsibility in publishing books.

# SATISFACTORY MANUSCRIPT

• All contracts provide that the manuscript must be "satisfactory" to the publisher before the publisher is required to pay the final portion of the advance typically payable on delivery of the manuscript and before the publisher is obligated to publish the book. This is a prerogative that a publisher understandably needs. However, be certain that the words "in form and content" are placed after "satisfactory" wherever the latter appears. This should eliminate the possibility of the publisher claiming that you have to return the advance simply because your topic is no longer popular or there are too many books on the subject at the time you deliver the manuscript. These are risks that the publisher properly takes.

## Return of Advance

1. You might want to try for a provision saying that if the publisher rejects the manuscript because it doesn't consider the manuscript "satisfactory in form and content," you won't be required to return the portion of the advance you already received unless and until you get another publisher (and another advance) for the book. In that situation, you agree to repay the first publisher from the advance you get

from the second. This saves you from having to repay money you may no longer have and eliminates the possibility that you were writing "on spec," i.e., writing with assurance neither of payment nor publication.

Some publishers will give you this provision. Among those that do, there may be some variations: some will require you to keep a part of the advance on this basis and return the rest immediately. Some may require you to repay the money within $x$ years even if you don't get another publisher. All, however, will require that the manuscript be timely delivered for this "first proceeds" provision to apply. All will also require that your delivered manuscript be subject to a "good faith" test, i.e., that you, in the publisher's opinion, delivered what you in good faith believed to be an acceptable manuscript and not something just to meet the delivery requirement.

2. If you are required to immediately return your advance because of nondelivery or because it was unsatisfactory, clarify that repayment of the advance by you is in full settlement—not in addition to—any other claims which the publisher may have because of nondelivery.

3. Because of disputes as to what is and is not a satisfactory manuscript requiring return of your advance, it is helpful to specify what you can about the nature of the manuscript and book. See the heading "The Manuscript— What to Deliver" above.

## Editor's Response

○      Ask for a provision requiring the publisher to notify you that your manuscript is accepted or give you written comments why it is not satisfactory (along with the opportunity to revise it) within $x$ days after you deliver the manuscript.

Provide that if the publisher does not do either by that deadline, then you may send the publisher a letter saying that the manuscript will be considered automatically accepted (and you will be entitled to that part of your advance due on acceptance) if the publisher does not accept the manuscript or give you written comments within $x$ days of your letter. This will avoid the problem of your handing in the manuscript and not hearing anything definitive, one way or the other, for an inordinately long period afterwards. In each case, 30-60 days would be appropriate for $x$, though the total for both should be 60-90 days,[5] not 90-120.

## Indexes

If you are required to deliver an index as part of the work, provide that its completion (or at least the insertion of page numbers, which cannot be done until the type has been set) is not a prerequisite to the manuscript being formally accepted.

# REPRESENTATIONS AND WARRANTIES

1. Carefully read this section of the contract and be sure you understand each statement that the publisher is asking you to make. (Representations and warranties are assurances by you that certain statements in the contract are true. "Representations" refer to their accuracy on the date of the contract; "warranties" are guarantees that the statements will remain true in the future. They are generally used interchangeably.)

• 2. Revise any statements that are incorrect so that they will be true.

3. In particular, check the option, noncompetition and "next book" clauses (see pages 54–59 below) in any other publishing contracts you may have signed to make sure that none of them prevent you from entering into the new contract. If you are obligated to show the manuscript to one of your previous publishers because of an option clause in an earlier contract and that book is still in print, fulfill that obligation first. If there are other questions or problems, consult with your agent or lawyer or call it to your new publisher's attention. If the earlier book is no longer in print, see what is required under the earlier contract to terminate that contract.

4. Ask the publisher to add, "These representations and warranties do not apply to any material furnished, or changes made, by the publisher" at the end of the section.

5. If you are granting rights to the publisher throughout the world (or for foreign languages) but your permissions from copyright holders of quoted material are only for the United States (or just for English-language editions), say so.

6. If you are signing the contract but are not the author, or will be working with a collaborator, be sure the publisher knows that. If you wrote the work for someone else while you were that person's employee, let the publisher know that too. (In that case, you may not have the right to enter into the contract).

7. If you have published any portion of the manuscript before—in a magazine, as a handout for students in a class you taught, or outside the United States, for example—let the publisher know that too so you and they can make whatever changes need to be made in the contract.

8. If you sign the contract and any of your representations or warranties are wrong, the publisher is not required to publish the book and can require you to return your advance. In addition, if the publisher is sued and loses because what you said is wrong, you will have to reimburse the publisher for its losses and pay its lawyers' fees too.

9. In certain cases, where you do not feel capable of making an unqualified statement, try to add "To my knowledge," or "To the best of my knowledge," at the start of the statement. This is often difficult to get, however.

10. Be careful about vague representations about the manuscript not violating "any other rights." Try to get the publisher to limit that clause to privacy, libel, publicity and obscenity.

# INDEMNIFICATION

Indemnification means that you have to reimburse the publisher for its losses and expenses if a representation or warranty made by you is wrong and the publisher is sued or loses money as a result.

When this occurs, you may also have to reimburse bookstores, distributors and others who bought your book from your publisher, if they were sued too. You will also have to pay the legal fees that your publisher and the others incurred in defending themselves. Most contracts provide that you have to reimburse these people not only if your representations and warranties are in fact wrong, but also if the publisher was sued because someone *claims* they were wrong, even if they were not and even if the publisher and you win the lawsuit.

If the publisher has insurance which protects the author, be sure that it is referred to in your contract. Also see if the deductible (the amount you have to pay before the insurance takes effect) offered by the publisher can be lowered.

The following comments assume that the publisher's insurance does not protect the author.[6]

○    1. Eliminate any reference in the indemnification section to "claims" and "allegations." You should properly reimburse the publisher if it loses money because your representations or warranties are wrong. But if someone merely *claims* that they are wrong, but they are not, you should not have to reimburse the publisher; that is a risk the publisher properly takes as a business enterprise.

Likewise, beware of the words "actions," "proceedings" and "lawsuits." You don't want to reimburse the publisher just because someone files a lawsuit; a lawsuit is little more than a formalized claim and does not mean that your representations were either right or wrong.

2. Instead, provide that you will indemnify the publisher only for "final judgments based upon a breach of any of the foregoing representations or warranties (and for all costs and expenses, including reasonable lawyers' fees, in connection therewith)." This means that a court would first have to decide that you were wrong before you were required to pay anything. Saying "final non-appealable judgment" instead of "final judgment" is even better because it means you would not have to pay unless the court's decision was upheld on appeal or it was decided not to appeal.

• 3. As an alternative, if the publisher balks at this, provide that if there is a lawsuit and you are found not to have violated your representations and warranties, then you and the publisher will split equally all costs involved. This is generally amenable to most publishers.

• 4. Also provide that the "Publisher will not settle any such claim, lawsuit or proceeding without Author's written consent, such consent not to be unreasonably withheld." This, however, is not necessary if the Publisher agrees that you are only required to indemnify it if there is a final court judgment that you breached your representation or warranty.

5. You may also be able to limit your maximum liability to the total amount of money earned and to be earned by you under the contract.

6. Since most contracts validly provide that the pub-

lisher may withhold all or part of your royalties if there is a claim or lawsuit concerning the book, ask for a provision requiring the publisher to review the status of the claim or lawsuit at least annually and to release the royalties if the claim or lawsuit is not being actively pursued. Also ask that any money withheld be placed in an interest-bearing account, the interest to be returned to you when the other money is returned or applied toward any indemnification required to be paid.

# RELATIONSHIP WITH OTHER CONTRACTS

o     1. Eliminate any reference to other publishing contracts that you may have with the same publisher which would allow the publisher to offset money you owe them under one contract against money earned on another. Each contract should stand on its own. (Language like this frequently appears in the indemnification section).

2. Be particularly careful about this on any contracts you do for a book producer where both you and the producer sign the same contract. You do not want any money which the producer owes on other books to be deducted from royalties paid on yours.

# PUBLICATION

- 1. Make sure there is an obligation for the publisher to publish the book and to do so within a specific period of time (e.g., 12 to 18 months from the manuscript's acceptance).
- 2. Add a provision that if they don't publish the book by that deadline, then (after you give them written notice and an additional $x$ months to do so), the contract terminates, all rights thereupon revert to you, and you keep all monies advanced *plus* any due upon publication.

## Changes in Manuscript

- Ask for a provision prohibiting changes in the manuscript or your illustrations without your approval, except for spelling, capitalization, punctuation and other grammatical changes required to conform to the publisher's style book. (E.g.: "Publisher will have the right to copyedit the manuscript to conform to its standard style in grammar, spelling and usage. No other change shall be made in the manuscript without the consent of the Author.")

## Title Approval

You might want to state that the work's tentative title, if

one is listed in the contract, will not be changed without your consent. Or that the title will be one satisfactory to both author and publisher.

## Cover Consultation or Approval

Approval of the cover design and text is very difficult to get. If it is important to you, you may be able to get the following provision which is of some help: "Publisher will show Author the sketches and designs for the Work's cover, as well as proofs thereof, in time for Author's suggestions and responses to be incorporated if Publisher agrees with them." More likely, if they give you anything, they will give you the right of "consultation," a vague word that is not terribly meaningful but better than nothing. As a practical matter in this area, you are best off being aware of your book's production schedule and, if you have a good relationship with your editor, trying to see the cover sketches and designs informally.

## Copyright Notice

1. Ask that the copyright be registered in your name. Virtually every publisher will agree to this.
2. Ask the publisher to insert a clause obligating them to print a proper copyright notice in the book in your name and requiring each licensee to do the same. Under copyright law, you will then be protected even if the publisher inadvertently neglects to print the proper notice.

# COPYRIGHT—"WORK FOR HIRE"

Some contracts may state that you are writing (or illustrating) the book on a "work for hire" basis or may categorize you as the publisher's "employee"; be wary about signing these. In those situations, the publisher will own the copyright and all other rights in the work. Among other things, that means that the publisher can do whatever it wishes with the work (including allowing others to adapt it for other media) without paying you any additional money.

There are circumstances when it is appropriate to do a book on a "work for hire" basis. Before doing so, however, be sure you understand the ramifications. If requested to do a book on a "work for hire" basis, and it is not a subject you are familiar with, discuss the matter with your agent or lawyer or contact Volunteer Lawyers for the Arts or The Authors Guild.[7]

# ADVANCE

## Amount

There is no magic formula to determine what the right amount is for an advance. Simply bear in mind that many publishers, however, are always willing to raise their initial offer. If the publisher's offer is less than what you want and you have a definite amount in mind, tell your editor the amount you want. If you feel awkward about doing this but would nonetheless like more than was offered, ask your editor, at the least, "How much higher can you go?" or "How much better can you do?" or "Is that the best you can do?"

Keep in mind that the amount of the advance can vary depending on what rights you are granting. An offer for world rights (hardcover and softcover, English and translations), including first serial and movie rights, should be higher than an offer just for United States English-language only rights, without first serial or dramatic rights.

A rule of thumb to keep in mind is to first discuss with your editor the number of copies they hope to sell in the first year and what price they expect to sell the book for. (The editor generally has this information because she/he prepared it before the company decided to make an offer for your book). Then, assuming a standard or expected royalty rate (see "Royalties" below), figure out what your royalty per book will be. Then multiply that by the number of copies expected to be sold in the first year. This will give you your total royalties for the first year if the book sold as well as the publisher hopes. Then, since books rarely do that well, figure that the publisher will give you an advance of roughly one-half to two-thirds that amount and be sure you get at least that as your advance.

> Example: The publisher expects to sell 10,000 copies of your book in the first year at $15 a copy. Your expected royalty rate, we are assuming, is 10% of the book's suggested retail price on the first 5,000 copies (i.e., $1.50 per book) and 12.5% on the next 5,000 ($1.875 per book). That means a total royalty of $7,500 (5,000 × $1.50) plus $9,375 (5,000 × $1.875), or a total of $16,875. Thus, your advance should be somewhere between $8,400 and $11,250. This is only a rough rule of thumb but many authors will find it helpful in establishing the minimum they should get. But don't be bashful about asking for more. The worst the publisher can say is "no."

Particularly if you are inexperienced, let the publisher make the first offer. They generally will, telling you what rights they want to buy, what they are offering as an advance and what they are offering as royalties. If you prefer not to negotiate for yourself, you can hire an agent or publishing lawyer to negotiate for you. An agent will charge 10-15% of whatever you get under the contract (advance, royalties and subsidiary rights) as his or her commission; lawyers generally charge by the hour (with a minimum fee in the event negotiations are concluded quickly or terminate without a contract).

# Timing

1. Advances are typically paid half on signing the contract (in reality, within 6-8 weeks after signing) and half when the author delivers the complete, "satisfactory"[8] manuscript. Occasionally, it is divided one-third on signing, one-third when half the manuscript is delivered and one-third when the completed (and satisfactory) manuscript is delivered.

2. Paperback houses frequently hold back a portion of the payment until the book is published. Although you should try to resist this, it is often unavoidable. If you do agree to that, however, include in your contract that the final payment                                              is to be made "when the Work is first published or within $x$ months from the date the manuscript is accepted, whichever comes first." This will prevent payment from being delayed if the promised publication date is delayed for reasons having nothing to do with you, a not unusual occurrence.

If a portion of the advance is held back until publication, provide that it will be paid to you immediately if, after the manuscript is accepted, the contract is terminated because of the publisher's failure to publish the work within the required time or for any reason other than a breach of author's representations or legal problems associated with the book.

# Bonuses

Bonuses (i.e., additional advances) are frequently negotiated by major authors writing major books. Examples are an additional $x,000 advance for each week the book appears on *The New York Times Book Review* bestseller list (generally with a maximum number of weeks) or if it hits number one on the *NYTBR* list or if a movie is made of the book. Keep in mind that these are still advances against royalties, not outright cash payments, and are not found in most contracts.

## Flow-through

Occasionally (and especially when one is dissatisfied with the size of the advance) an author asks for a provision requiring accelerated payment of certain subsidiary rights income. This "flow-through" clause is not particularly easy to get but is obtainable, especially for rights which are normally withheld by an author's agent. See "Subsidiary Rights— When Paid" on page 44.

## Miscellaneous

Some authors like to include the following clause to guard against publishers unexpectedly charging the author for expenses generally considered the publisher's responsibility:

> "Other than as specifically provided in this Agreement,[9] no amounts paid or payable by the Publisher in connection with the Work may be deducted from Author's advance, royalties or any other monies payable to Author under this Agreement."

With major publishers, however, this is generally not necessary though few would object to adding it.

It can also be helpful to add the following:

"Except in connection with any breach of Author's representations and warranties, or as otherwise specifically provided in this Agreement[10], the advance shall not be repayable."[11]

# ROYALTIES

• 1. Make sure your contract specifies whether your royalty is based on a percentage of the book's suggested retail price (also called the "list" price) or on its "net" price. The difference is important.

"Net" is the amount that the publisher receives from the bookstore, wholesaler or other persons to whom it sells the book and is generally 40-50% less than the retail price. Thus, a 10% royalty based on list, for a book which retails for $10, will earn the author $1 per book. A 10% royalty based on net, however, would be 60 cents per book on copies sold to bookstores (which typically get a 40% discount and therefore buy a $10 book for $6) and 52 cents on copies sold to wholesalers (who often receive a 48% discount, buying the book for $5.20). Textbooks (and scholarly and scientific books from university presses and specialized publishing houses) are typically sold to bookstores at a 20% discount.[12] A contract that says royalties are based on the "amount received" by the publisher is a royalty based on net.

Most established trade book publishers (i.e., publishers of fiction or nonfiction books intended for a general audience) base their royalties on list, and it is generally advantageous to the author to do so. Textbook publishers, university presses, small presses and specialty publishers usually base their royalties on net. Royalties based on net can work out

28

perfectly well if the guidelines listed on pages 31–33 are followed. However, publishers that base royalties on net frequently pay less per book in royalties than those basing royalties on list.

o     2. Be sure that royalty rates are specified for both hardcover and softcover editions (unless the specified rate is for "all books" or for "books"). If the publisher is one of the handful that publishes mass market and trade paperbacks, be sure to specify royalties for each type.

This is especially important when the publisher initially plans to publish only a paperback edition and therefore specifies only the lower paperback rate in its contract, even though you are licensing hardcover rights to the publisher in your contract also.

3. Except in "work for hire" arrangements, you should always be getting royalties (with, hopefully, an advance against those royalties) and not just a lump sum payment without royalties.[13]


## "Standard" Royalty Rates

•     1. Generally speaking, an author should expect or seek the royalties (based on list) stated below for fiction or nonfiction books published by established trade publishers. A publisher's initial offer is frequently lower; if you are offered less, negotiate hard. Keep in mind that these are only minimums, and that established authors (and "ordinary" authors who are very good negotiators) can occasionally do better.

**Hardcover** (other than children's books): You should get 10% of list on the first 5,000 copies sold, 12-1/2% of list on the next 5,000 copies, and 15% of list on all copies sold thereafter. Sometimes the first increase (also called "escalation") is at 7,500 or 10,000 copies. A royalty rate higher than 15% of list is rare.

**Trade Paperback**:[14] With established trade publishers, royalties should be at least 6% of list on the first 10,000-25,000 copies and 7-1/2% afterwards. However, you should try for 7-1/2% of list on all copies with, if possible, an increase to 10% after somewhere between 25,000 and 100,000 copies are sold; a few major paperback houses refuse to jump to 10%, however. Note that there are certain publishers—primarily small presses and some publishers of Christian books—who predominantly publish trade paperbacks rather than hardcovers and pay royalties on trade paperbacks equal to the standard hardcover royalties cited in the previous paragraph.

**Mass Market Paperbacks**: Some publishers still try to give royalties of 6% of list on the first $x$ (e.g., 150,000) copies and 8% afterwards; this is low. Try for royalties of at least 8% of list on the first $x$ number of copies sold and 10% on all copies sold thereafter. On royalties of 8%/10%, the typical "break point" is 150,000 copies.

**Children's Hardcover Books**: The typical royalty is 10% of list, without an escalator clause. On picture books and other heavily illustrated books, this is generally divided half to the author and half to the illustrator. It is also sometimes possible, with certain publishers, to obtain an escalation to 12-1/2% of list after 10,000 or more copies.

**Children's Paperback Books**: The typical royalty is 6% of list, although some publishers try to pay 5% of list and some will pay the same 10% of list as if it were a hardcover book.

**Textbooks**: Although "standard" royalties are less common in this field, typical initial royalties range between 10% and 15% of net, with royalties between 15% of net and 15% of list reportedly being fairly standard on sales of more than 5,000 copies. There is little reason why textbook authors should not strive for the same 10%/12.5%/15% (of list) that authors of hardcover trade books get. (Assuming a 20% average discount, this would correspond to 12.5%/15.625%/18.75% of net.) Textbook authors should also try for the escalation to 15% of list at 5,000 copies, with the increase from 10% to 12.5% perhaps occurring at 2,500 copies.

○   2. Always try for an "escalation" clause, i.e., an increase in royalties after a specified number of copies of sold. If a publisher refuses to give it, find out how many copies the publisher expects to sell and ask for the increase after that point.[15] Keep in mind that most of a publisher's fixed costs are associated with initially typesetting, producing and publicizing the book; royalties are generally lower on the initial $x,000 copies sold to enable the publisher to attempt to recoup those expenses. Since these expenses typically do not recur on subsequent printings, the publisher is better able to give you a higher royalty on those sales.

Note that the "break" points at which the royalties increase are as important a part of the negotiations as the royalty rate.

## Net, Royalties Based On

1. Keep in mind that when royalties are based on net, they are generally 20-50% less than what they would be if

based on list. Thus, to equal a "standard" royalty based on list, percentages based on net have to be higher.

For example, if the average discount to bookstores and wholesalers is 50%, 20% of net is the same as 10% of list. If the average discount is 40%, 16-2/3% of net is the same as 10% of list. If the average discount is 20%, 12-1/2% of net is the same as 10% of list.

Many publishers, especially smaller ones and university presses, like to use net because they find it easier from a bookkeeping standpoint. In dealing with publishers which compute royalties on net, ask them what their average discount is on books sold by them. Then figure out the rate you need, as a percentage of net, to equate with the percentages of list mentioned under "Standard Royalty Rates" above. A table of equivalencies between royalties based on list and those based on net is in Note 12 at the end of this book.

2. When royalties are based on net because the publisher assures you that they only sell at a 20% discount (called a "short" discount), it is helpful to get the publisher's written agreement that if any books are sold at more than 20% off, they will nonetheless be treated for royalty purposes as if sold for only 20% off. This will protect you from a change in publisher's policy from a short to a full discount or any other change in its discount policy.[16]

3. Using the term "net" without defining it can create problems because net is itself shorthand for "an amount net of certain specified items." As an author, you want to be sure that none of the publisher's expenses for paper, printing, binding, production or sales costs are deducted in reaching "net."[17] If "net" is used, ask that it be defined in one of two ways:

a. "As used in this Agreement, 'net' means the publisher's suggested retail list price for the book less the discount provided by the publisher to its customer." or

b. "As used in this Agreement, 'net income' means all monies payable to the Publisher from the sale or licensing of the Work pursuant to this Agreement. In determining 'net income' for purposes of the royalty and licensing percentage sections of this Agreement, shipping, handling and insurance charges, and sales and similar taxes shall be excluded."

4. When the contract says that royalties (or percentages of subsidiary rights) are based on "amount received" or the publisher's "receipts," the author may not get royalties on books sold by the publisher if the publisher is unable to collect its bill.[18] Bad debt and credit problems, however, are traditional business operating risks that publishers should properly assume; they are not an author's responsibility.

If your contract uses "amount received" by the publisher or a similar phrase, ask that it either be changed to "amount payable" to the publisher or that the term be defined in the same way as we have just suggested "net income" be defined. In addition, add this at the end of the definition: "There shall be no reduction in royalties or 'amount received' because of nonpayment by customers."

## "Deep Discount"

• 1. When the basic royalty is based on list, be very careful about a clause in most contracts that provides for a reduced royalty when the publisher sells copies at more than a specified discount (i.e., at a "deep discount") from the book's suggested retail price. These clauses accomplish the reduction by either lowering the percentage figure from that specified for royalties on "regular" sales or by switching the calculation from a percentage of list to a percentage of amount received (i.e., "net").

In these "deep discount" situations, some reduction in royalty amount is often appropriate because the increased discount does produce a smaller profit for the publisher. However, the solutions offered in many contracts are terribly unfair to the author. Because of higher-than-usual discounts demanded by certain wholesalers, independent distributors and chains, you could find that more books are being sold at a sharply-diminished royalty rate—frequently less than half the regular rate—rather than the full rate.[19]

The worst version of this clause is one that provides that whenever copies are sold at a discount of 48% or greater, the applicable royalty rate for those copies is changed to 10% of *net* (even when the contract provides for escalating royalties of 10%/12.5%/15% based on list for regular sales). In this situation (assuming a book retailing for $10 and enough copies sold for the 15% royalty rate to be in effect), a book sold to a wholesaler at 50% off (i.e., for $5) will yield a royalty of 50 cents to the author rather than $1.50. And this notwithstanding that the increased cost to the publisher for a sale at 50% on a $10 book, as opposed to a sale at 47% when the full royalty applies, is only 30 cents more. (Yes, the author loses a dollar but the publisher actually gains 70 cents overall!)

The solutions that are fairest to the author, in approximate order of preference, are:

> a. Specify that the deep discount clause only applies on "sales outside ordinary wholesale and retail trade channels" or to "sales other than to wholesalers, distributors, bookstores and other retail outlets where books are traditionally sold." A

34

simple way to do this is to add the phrase "(except for sales through ordinary wholesale and retail book trade channels)" immediately after the percentage specified by the publisher in the contract as triggering the reduced royalty provisions.

b. Change the percentage which triggers the reduced royalty clause to 51% or 52% (in the case of hardcovers and trade paperbacks) and to 55% or 60% (in the case of mass market paperbacks). In this regard, be careful of nuances like "at $x\%$ or more" and "more than $x\%$"; if many sales are at exactly $x\%$, the difference between the two can be substantial. Thus, even a change from "50% or more" to "more than 50%" can be helpful.[20]

c. Provide that the then-prevailing "regular" royalty rate will decrease by 1/2% for every percentage point that the discount given by the publisher to its customer exceeds the percentage discount which triggers the reduction of royalty (with a minimum royalty of one-half the original). For example, if the triggering percentage is 50% and the books are sold at 53% off, the author's royalty would be 1.5% [53%–50%=3; 3 × 1/2%=1.5%] less than the royalty rate in effect at that time (i.e., 11% if the book was then getting regular royalties at a 12.5% rate). In this way, the increased discount that the publisher gives the wholesaler is shared equally between the author and the publisher.

A variation of this that most publishers readily accept is that if the triggering percentage (often 50%) is exceeded, then the author and publisher share the loss equally but base the amount of the loss on the difference between the discount at which the books were sold (53% in our example) and 44%

(instead of the 50% triggering percentage). In our example, this would mean that a 9% (53 minus 44) decrease is shared, and that the author's royalty in effect at the time would decrease by 4-1/2% (from 12.5% of list to 8% of list in our example).[21,22]

    d. Specify that the same escalating royalty percentages you negotiated for regular sales will apply to deep discount sales but, for the deep discount sales, will be based on net rather than on the book's list price. At the least, this will help limit your losses when you have escalating royalties and are no longer in the lowest category.[23]

In negotiating deep discounts, both sides should understand that the deep discount provision was originally inserted in contracts for "special sales" such as premiums. In these situations, the publisher has the opportunity to sell a large number of books, at a small percentage over cost and on a nonreturnable basis, to a purchaser not in the book business and where it is not expected that the books will end up in bookstores. The purchaser then gives the book away or sells the book at a very low price to people who buy the product (e.g., razors or lawn fertilizer) it manufactures. Most publisher's deep discount provisions are basically fair for special sales like these; unfortunately, however, many contracts do not clearly limit the clause to special sales but instead just use a percentage number as the criterion.

    2. Whichever alternative you end up with, be sure to specify that the author's royalty shall never be less than half the otherwise-applicable royalty rate (except for "special sales," where the sales are not made to bookstores or wholesalers.)[24]

    3. Specify that copies sold from small printings (see below) and copies sold to wholesalers and bookstores on which

reduced royalties are payable because of deep discount provisions will nonetheless be included in the number of books sold for purposes of computing applicable royalties if your contract provides for an escalating rate of royalty based on the number of books sold.

## Other Reduced Royalties

Read carefully and understand every provision where the publisher can pay less than the full royalty. Consider whether any of the publisher's exceptions to full royalty should not apply to your situation.

Some contracts provide for reduced royalties on sales to computer stores, gift stores, religious stores, and gourmet food stores. If you have written a computer book, a cook book or a religious book, however, and if the publisher sells to these stores with its regular sales force at standard discounts, there is no reason for your royalty to be trimmed.

○ **Small Printings**: When there is a provision in the contract providing for reduced royalties from small printings (e.g., 1,000 or 2,500 copies), add two points if they are not already there (they frequently are not): (i) the clause does not apply to the book's first printing; and (ii) the reduced royalty only applies if the total number of books sold by the publisher during the calendar year in question is less than the number specified in the contract as constituting a "small" printing. (Thus, you would get full royalties if the book sold 6,000 copies during the year even if the publisher only printed 1,000 at a time but did so six times). An alternative to this second point, but less favorable to the author, would be to provide that the provision cannot be utilized more than once in any 12-month period.

Publishers will also, if requested, frequently lower the number of copies which constitutes a small printing (especially if the number in their contract is more than 1,000 copies) and increase the size of the reduced royalty from one-half the regular royalty rate (for example) to two-thirds or three-quarters.

**Reprints**: Some contracts specify a lower royalty for reprint, "cheap" or "lower price" editions. When there, it is intended for lower-price hardcover reprints, not softcover, and the word "hardcover" should be inserted in the clause before the word "reprint" (or after "cheap" or "lower price") to make that clear. Prudent authors will also define "lower price" as $x\%$ (at least 50%) less than the original trade hardcover.

**Mail Order**: This should be defined as "mail order direct to the consumer" to preclude its use for reduced royalties on library sales.

# SUBSIDIARY RIGHTS

## Introduction; List of Rights

Subsidiary rights are rights an author grants to the publisher in addition to the right to initially publish the book. In general (with important exceptions), the publisher does not exercise these rights itself. Instead it licenses them to others and shares the money it gets with the author.

There are two facets to subsidiary rights: (i) what subsidiary rights you are granting and (ii) how the money received from licensing these rights will be split between author and publisher.

The following are the subsidiary rights typically granted by all authors to the publisher:

1. To license others to reprint the book (in paperback or in hardcover).

2. To license book club editions of the book.

3. To serialize portions of the book in magazines and newspapers after the book's publication ("second serial" rights).

4. To license others to abridge and condense the book and to include the work in anthologies or otherwise quote from it.

5. To license others to publish the book for use as "premiums."

6. To license nondramatic recorded readings

(although this may soon become a right typically withheld by authors with agents).

7. For publicity purposes, to allow others (without charge) to quote from the book in print or on radio or television so long as the portion quoted is less than $x$ words (e.g., 2,000).

The following are subsidiary rights generally retained by authors who have literary agents capable of licensing these rights themselves or through subagents; in that situation, money received from licensing is not shared with the publisher.

1. To publish English-language editions of the book in England and other members of the Commonwealth of Nations (except for Canada).

2. To license translations into foreign languages.

3. Performance Rights (i.e., movies, plays, animation, television, cable, videocassettes, etc.).

4. "First Serial" rights (the right to publish excerpts from the book in magazines and newspapers *before* the book is initially published by the book publisher).

5. To adapt the book for use in computer databases and software (although not all agents withhold these).

6. Audio recording rights (e.g., records, tapes, audiocassettes and compact discs).

## Points to Watch Out for—General

The important items to remember about subsidiary rights are:

- 1. Be specific in listing what rights you are granting. Be particularly careful about the word "including" immediately after a general term; in such instances "including" is typically followed by a long list of rights. When this occurs, delete both the general term and the word "including." List only the specific rights that you are willing to grant; any others should be crossed out.

  Remember that it is particularly important in reading a contract, whenever confronted by a long list of items separated by commas and semicolons, to analyze every item carefully and to avoid the normal tendency to quickly scan the list and assume it is okay.

  In this regard, note that "electronic" and "mechanical" are vague terms and should generally be avoided. If the publisher intends to have the rights for computer databases, audiocassettes, videocassettes, phonograph records and the like, it should specify them. (You should always know what you are and are not granting. Otherwise, if another company approaches you to exploit rights that are not specified, you may not know if you are entitled to license them separately.)

○ 2. If you are allowing the publisher to license foreign translations of your book or English-language editions in England and other Commonwealth countries[25]—either because you don't have an agent or the agent agreed to license "world rights" to the publisher—include a clause that requires those rights to revert to you for any country or language where the publisher does not license them within $x$ years (3-5) after the book's initial publication in the United States. Similarly, if you are granting any other rights to the publisher that are typically kept by the author when the author has an agent, ask that those rights too revert to you if not licensed by the publisher within 3-5 years after the book's initial publication.

- 3. Be particularly wary about anything that says or implies that you are granting "commercial" or "merchandis-

41

ing" rights (e.g., T-shirts, decals, lunch boxes, games, dolls, etc.). With very few exceptions, these should never be included in a publishing contract, and few publishers insist on them. If the publisher wants them, there should be a separate contract with different termination dates, performance guaranties and other special provisions appropriate to merchandising agreements.[26]

•    4. Be careful nothing in the contract's language grants any right to characters, names, situations, prequels, sequels or series. Even when granting performance rights, you should not allow the publisher to license rights to characters, sequels, prequels or the like. If you think anything in the publisher's contract might imply a grant of any of these rights, cross it out or negate the implication with specific language to the contrary.[27] Again, few publishers will have difficulty with this concept.

5. If you are granting book rights to the publisher only in certain countries and territories, then the grant of subsidiary rights should be limited to those same countries and territories. Your contract should be clear on this.

6. Although income from paperback reprint licenses is typically split 50/50 between hardcover publisher and author, provide that you get 100% of the income (royalties and advances) if your hardcover publisher prints the paperback edition itself or licenses paperback rights to an affiliated company.

7. Specify that if the publisher hires agents to find licensees for certain subsidiary rights (or lawyers to negotiate the contracts), commissions and fees paid to these people will be deducted from the publisher's share of any proceeds.

8. Ask to be promptly notified of any licenses granted. Also ask that copies of the licensing agreements (at least on major rights) be given to you if you ask for them.

9. See point 1 under "Grant of Rights" about carefully reading the contract's language. It applies here too.

# Income

### Division with Publisher

The income from most subsidiary rights licensed by the publisher is generally split 50/50 between author and publisher. There are, however, a handful of exceptions, mainly relating to rights that are frequently withheld by an agent when the author is represented by one. The typical exceptions to a 50/50 split are listed below. (In all cases, these percentage splits assume that any amounts paid by the publisher for any agents or lawyers it hires to help with the transaction are deducted from the publisher's share).

*First serial rights*: 90% to author and 10% to publisher.

*British Commonwealth rights*: 75-80% to author, 20-25% to publisher.

*Translation rights*: 75% to author, 25% to publisher. Authors and illustrators of children's books should also seek these percentages although some publishers insist on a split closer to 50/50.

*Performance rights* (including recording and videocassette rights): 90% to author, 10% to publisher.

*Computer rights* (information storage, manipulation and retrieval rights): There are no definitive standards here yet. With some publishers it is 50/50; with others, it can be 80%/20% in favor of the author.

*Paperback rights*: Although 50/50 is the norm, it is occasionally possible to negotiate better splits, e.g., 70%/30% (rare) or 60%/40%. One variation that publishers are increasingly willing to give is a 60%/40% split on all amounts received in excess of $100,000. (See, however, point 6 on page 42).

*Merchandising*: As noted, this should not be granted in a publishing contract for a variety of reasons. If, in spite of this, you have been convinced to do so, the split should be better than 50/50. In addition, it is essential to provide that if the publisher hires a licensing agent, his or her share comes out of the publisher's share.

Most authors and publishers consider the splits listed above as fair to both. If you are granting these rights and not getting the indicated splits, you should ask for them.

## When Paid (Flow-through)

Typically, money from licensing subsidiary rights in the book is paid to the author with his or her next regular royalty check, which can be as much as nine months after the publisher received the money. Requiring that the money instead be paid to the author within $x$ days (e.g., 30) after the publisher gets it is called "flow-through" or "pass-through," i.e., the author's share flows directly through to the author without the normal delays.

There are two types of flow-through. The more typical, and the one easier to get, requires these accelerated payments to be made only after the author's advance has "earned out."[28] The other allows the payments to be made as additional advances even if the advance has not earned out at the time; this version is particularly difficult to get but is occasionally agreed to as a compromise on contracts for major authors when the advance is significantly lower than the author wanted.

When given, flow-through is more apt to be given for those rights not usually granted to the publisher but which are generally withheld by the agent. However, in certain situations authors can also get it for book club rights and even paperback rights. Provided that the advance has already earned out, there is little logic on the publisher's side for rejecting this position.

Whatever the case, flow-through clauses should only apply when the author's share of the money is more than a specified minimum amount (e.g., $1,000) so the publisher is not burdened with the bookkeeping chores when only small amounts are involved (as with permission fees for quoting brief excerpts from the book, for example).

## More About Certain Rights

The following comments regarding particular subsidiary rights may be helpful if they apply to your situation.

*Adaptations, Abridgments and Condensations*: If you want the right to approve any of these, whether done by the original publisher or a licensee, say so in the contract.

*Series*: If what you have is an idea for a series (even if it may not involve the same characters or setting), clarify whether you or the publisher has the rights to do other books in the series. If there is a slogan or series title, in whose name will it be trademarked? If the publisher does other books in the series, will you get anything for those? If you think your book falls in any of these categories, discuss the points with your editor and make sure the contract reflects your agreement.

*Performance Rights*: If you are granting these, you may still want to require that you see drafts of all agreements and options on a timely basis and have your comments incorporated (i.e., right of comment and approval). This could affect the type of credit you get on any productions of the work and whether you will have a consultant's role or a chance to be involved in the script.

*Sound Reproduction*: If you are granting these rights for

records and cassettes, be sure the language does not include the rights for soundtracks of dramatizations or the sound portions of videocassettes and the like. These rights are typically licensed with the movie or stage rights.

*Reprint Rights*: Bear in mind that this is a broad term and includes both hardcover (deluxe editions and special remainder editions) and softcover (mass market and trade paperback) editions.

*Serialization*: If there is a different split for first and second serial rights, you may want to provide that if the book is sold for publication in more than one installment and the first such publication is before the book's initial publication, then all installments will be deemed to be prior to the book's initial publication (i.e., first serial).

*Cartoon Rights*: If these are specified, add "book" after "cartoon" if you wish to retain the rights for licensing newspaper comic strips while allowing the publisher the right to do a book version.

*Calendars*: If a calendar can be developed from your book, clarify who has the right to do this and what royalties will be paid if the publisher does it itself.

*Approval Rights*: Some contracts may provide that the author has the right to approve reprint (paperback) and foreign rights licenses. While helpful to have, this can be difficult to obtain and is not customary.

# ROYALTY STATEMENTS

Most trade book contracts provide for royalty statements every six months, accompanied by a check if the statement indicates that monies are due. This is fair. University press and other contracts frequently provide for annual statements and payments; six months is preferable.

Statements are typically issued 90 days after the end of the six-month accounting period. Some publishers try to stretch this to 120 days, which gives them the free use of your money for four months. This should be resisted, particularly with very small publishers whose accounting is not that complex.

Provide that you receive a royalty statement for as long as the contract is in effect. (Most contracts provide that you get a statement only as long as royalties are above a certain minimum amount.)[29] A statement that the money won't be paid to you unless the total royalties owed is above that minimum, generally $10 or $25, is okay.

• You should get a royalty statement and royalties, if owed, even if the book is initially published in the middle of a royalty period. Some publishers' contracts provide that you are not entitled to a statement and royalties until the book has been available for a full (i.e., six-month) royalty period or if it was published during the last two months of a period. This is unfair. The publisher is protected from paying royalties on

47

books subsequently returned by a "reserve for returns" clause.

The publisher is entitled to withhold a reasonable reserve for returns and the contract will say that (though be sure the word "reasonable" is there). You should ask, however, that the amount of the reserve withheld (in dollar amount and number of books) be specified on your royalty statement or in an accompanying letter. Failing that, provide that the publisher will furnish you this information "upon request."

Some publishers, though not many, will also agree in the contract not to withhold reserves on any books sold more than $x$ years previously (e.g., 18 months to 3 years).

Be careful that nothing in the contract provides, directly or by inference, that you do not get royalties on books that the publisher sells but does not get paid for. See point 4 under "Royalties—Net."

Older contracts sometimes have a provision limiting the maximum amount of earnings payable to you in any one year. If this is in your contract, delete it; it relates to provisions of the tax law that no longer apply.

# TERMINATION

• Be sure there is a section in the contract which provides that the contract will terminate in the following situations:

a. Failure of the publisher to publish the book within a specified time (1 year to 18 months is generally fair to both parties) after the manuscript is accepted (or treated as accepted as set forth under "Satisfactory Manuscript—Editor's Response"), provided that the author has first given the publisher written notice of its failure and an additional $x$ days (e.g., 90) to do so.

b. If a petition under the bankruptcy laws is filed by the publisher, or if the publisher admits in writing its inability to pay its debts when they become due or makes an assignment of its assets for the benefit of its creditors or otherwise liquidates its business, or if a court determines that the publisher is legally bankrupt.[30]

c. When the book goes out of print (see below).

A material breach of the contract by the publisher, not remedied by the publisher after 60 days written notice from the author, should also be reason for termination. Most publishers, however, refuse to add that to their contracts.

# OUT OF PRINT

o    It is important to define this term. Simply saying "when the Work goes out of print" or "when the Book is no longer in print" is too vague, especially when the contract grants foreign and nonbook subsidiary rights to the publisher. The definition itself should refer to (and be limited to) sales of:

a. the book;
b. in an English-language edition;
c. in the United States;
d. being offered for sale through bookstores; and
e. being available in sufficient quantities for such sales.

A fair definition would be that "The Work shall be considered 'in print' only when copies of an English-language book edition are regularly available and offered for sale in the United States by the Publisher or its licensee in sufficient quantities for general distribution to bookstores." Adding the phrase "and the book is included in the Publisher's or its licensee's annual catalog" at the end of this definition is also helpful if the publisher is willing to include it.

It would be even better if you can get a clause saying that if fewer than $x$ copies of the English-language book edition are sold in the United States in any year, or if your royalties during any year from sales of the book in the United States are less than $x$ dollars, then the contract will terminate. Publishers, however, are loath to give either of these.

# EFFECT OF TERMINATION

The contract should specify what happens on termination of the contract. Although some of these may be implicit, it is helpful to make everything clear. The following should be listed as ramifications of the contract's termination:

a. All rights granted by the contract automatically revert to the author.

b. The author keeps all monies previously paid by the publisher (as advances, royalties or payment of subsidiary rights income) and remains entitled to get any amounts still owing (including any advances payable upon initial publication of the book, if that is how the advance was structured). The only exception to this is if the contract was terminated because of the author's failure to deliver the manuscript, if the manuscript was rejected as unsatisfactory or if any of the author's representations or warranties were subsequently found to be false.

c. The publisher remains obligated to pay royalties to the author on any copies of the book in publisher's stock that it subsequently sells.

d. For $x$ days after termination (60 days is fair), the author can buy the film or plates used in printing the book from the publisher at a price tied to the cost of the film or the plates. (This price, which should be stated in the contract, ranges between the scrap value of the material at the time of termination to the publisher's cost of making the film; 50% of publisher's cost, exclusive of typesetting, is frequently acceptable to both sides).

You should also provide for your right to buy all or a portion of the publisher's overstock of your book at the lesser of *a)* publisher's cost (exclusive of typesetting) or *b)* the price at which the publisher intends to sell them to a "remainder" book company. Include a clause requiring the publisher to notify you, *x* days before any such sale, of the price it has been offered for the books.

# OPTION

Option clauses give your publisher the right to publish your next book under certain circumstances. Although some authors don't believe in granting them, there is little risk in giving this clause if the following changes are made in the publisher's standard clause.

- 1. The publisher's contract will generally say that you must submit your next work (or the manuscript for your next work) to your publisher before you submit it to another publisher. Change this so that all you are required to submit is an outline for the work plus one sample chapter (or, at most, two sample chapters). This is enough for a publisher to decide whether it wants to offer you a contract.

- 2. Be careful when the option period starts. The "standard" clause often says that the publisher will have $x$ weeks to consider your new work but that this period will not start until $x$ weeks *after* your current book is published, regardless of when you submit the outline and sample chapter. This is unacceptable since the date of publication is within the publisher's control. You should not have to wait until the first book is out before learning whether the publisher wants your second book or whether you have to start seeking another publisher. To remedy this, provide that the option period starts $x$ weeks (four is reasonable) after your current manuscript is *accepted* by the publisher in accordance with the contract.

3. Be sure to specify a period (4-5 weeks is fair to both) after the date you submit the outline and sample chapter during which the publisher must tell you if it wants to exercise its option. Provide that if you hear nothing during that period, then the publisher will be considered to have refused its option and you are free to submit your outline or manuscript to others.

4. Provide that if the publisher tells you it wants your work, then you and it will negotiate in good faith the terms of a new contract. Do not provide that the terms of the contract will be the same as your current one. As an author with a book already accepted for publication, your next book should be more valuable than the current one.

5. Provide that you and the publisher will negotiate the terms of the new contract for $x$ weeks (six is fair) and that if agreement is not reached within that time, you are free to approach and sign with other publishers.

6. The "standard" contract may provide that if your publisher wants the book but cannot reach agreement with you on the terms, then you can go elsewhere but only on financial terms that are the same or better than those offered to your first publisher. If this language is in your contract, delete the word "financial" before "terms" since there are more terms to a contract than financial ones and there are considerations other than money in choosing a publisher.

7. If there is a provision saying that even if you go elsewhere, the first publisher has the right to match any other offer you get, delete that phrase. You will just be wasting the time of a second publisher (and your own) if, after you reach a contract with the second one, the first can say "I want it after all."

8. If you are an author who does many books for different publishers, you may wish to limit the option to your next book that is similar to the current one, e.g., your next biography or your next novel (or your next textbook, next nonfiction book, next book involving the same lead character, etc.). If you are writing under a pseudonym, you may wish to limit the clause to your next book published under that pseudonym.

9. You may wish to exclude from the option situations where you are asked to collaborate, as the writer, with a celebrity or with a person who has a particular expertise but lacks the time or skill to write the book alone. You may also want to try to exclude situations where another publisher approaches you with the idea for a book.

10. If you are writing the book with a collaborator, clarify whether the option covers books written by each of you separately or only both of you together. And make sure the option is for only one book—i.e., not your next book *and* your collaborator's next book *and* your next joint effort.[31]

# COMPETITIVE BOOKS

o    Most contracts, particularly for nonfiction books, prohibit an author from publishing a "competitive" book without the publisher's consent. "Competitive," however, is a very broad term. Without clarification, it will be difficult later to be certain which books you can publish without your publisher's consent and which you cannot. If possible, eliminate the clause entirely on the grounds that unless the publisher will agree not to publish competitive books, you should not be prohibited either. Although logical, this is (for good reason from a publisher's viewpoint) rarely accepted.

A good alternative is to narrow the word's scope as much as possible. If your book is a textbook, say that only "competitive textbooks" are prohibited; then it will be clear that you will be permitted to publish a book on the same topic for a lay audience. If the textbook is an introductory one (e.g., for nursing or economics), clarify that you are not prohibited from publishing textbooks that are expansions of individual chapters in the book or are written for advanced courses. As much as possible, try to narrow the clause by describing what kind of book would be competitive, e.g., "a work on the same subject directed to the same audience and treated in the same manner and depth." Also specify that the clause applies only to books and not to articles or other subsidiary rights. It can also be helpful to state that the clause is limited to the same language, geographic area and markets for which you are granting rights.

If the book is fiction, however, many publishers will delete the clause as inapplicable and rely on the option clause to give the publisher the protection it needs.

○ If the book is fiction and you are not able to get the clause deleted in its entirety, be particularly careful to provide that subsequent works involving the same character, e.g., sequels, will not be considered competitive. Or, if they are, that you will still be permitted to publish them elsewhere if first offered to your publisher under your contract's option clause and no contract results; in that situation, provide that no future works involving the same character or situation will thereafter be considered competitive either.

It is also often possible to provide that the clause only applies for the first $x$ years (e.g., 3-4) after the book's initial publication. This is helpful.

# "NEXT BOOK" CLAUSES

Some contracts provide that the book under contract will be the next book you are doing for any publisher. While relatively innocuous, it can cause problems for professional writers who work on several projects at once. It could also prevent you from legally entering into contracts for new books while you are working on the current one if the delivery dates for the manuscripts conflict. If you keep the clause, make sure it is limited to your agreement to not deliver a manuscript for another book before the delivery date for the one in question.

# REVISED EDITIONS

The easiest way to handle this section of a contract is to say that no revisions to the work are permitted without the consent of both author and publisher. In most cases, this will be enough to protect both author and publisher. In the nonfiction area, however, publishers frequently want the right to get someone to revise the book if the author chooses not to (or cannot) do the revision. This is necessary for the publisher when dealing with directories, textbooks and certain basic reference books.

The typical clause provides that the publisher can get someone else to prepare the new edition and pay that person with monies otherwise payable to you as royalties or advances on the new edition. However, authors should make sure the following points are covered to protect themselves.

1. It should be clear that you have the first opportunity to revise the book, or to get someone to do it under your supervision, before the publisher can get someone else.

• 2. Provide that even if the publisher gets someone else, the amount of money that can be paid to that person from monies otherwise payable to you should be limited. Figures acceptable to many publishers are these: if the edition is the first that you have not worked on, then up to 50% of royalties otherwise payable to you on that edition can be paid to the person doing the revision; if the revision is the second you have not worked on, then up to 75% of monies otherwise payable to you can be used; and if it is the third or more that you haven't worked on, then up to 90% can be used.

Few publishers' standard contracts provide any limitation on the amount of your money that can be used. This is unfair. The book that is selling is basically yours, even if someone else is updating it. Thus, you are entitled to continuing royalties. And placing no limitation on the amount payable to the reviser means the publisher has no incentive to be conservative in the money it pays for revisions since it is paying the reviser with your money, not its own.

3. Require that any contract entered into by the publisher with the reviser be on a "work for hire" or similar basis which provides that the reviser will have no rights in the work other than to receive the agreed-upon compensation for the edition being revised. This will avoid future disputes about ownership of copyright, rights to make future revisions and reversion of rights if and when the work goes out of print. The contract with the reviser should also make it clear that these rights are yours, not the publisher's (in both cases, subject to the terms of your contract), since it is basically your money that is being used to pay the reviser. You may also wish to require that any contract with a third party be entered into only after "arms-length" negotiations (see page 64) to make sure that particularly favorable terms are not given to a friend or employee of the publisher's.

4. You may wish to include a clause stating that if you are unable to do revisions because you are dead, the publisher must offer your estate or literary executor the opportunity to hire someone to prepare the revision. This will enable your estate to determine how much the reviser will get and keep for your heirs the bulk of the royalties for the book you originated.

5. Require that your name appear on any revised edition

of the book. Provide that if you (or your estate) get someone to work on the revised edition, then it is your (or your estate's) decision whether that person will be listed as a coauthor. Provide that if the publisher hires the person to revise the work, the revision will be submitted to you for approval and that if you don't like the revision, you have the right to have your name deleted as an author. Discuss what type of credit (coauthor? equal billing?) the publisher is permitted to give to the reviser.

6. You may wish to provide for an additional advance whenever you are requested to prepare a revised edition of your book.

7. Consider whether you want a provision prohibiting the publisher from revising the work more than once every $x$ years without your consent. Otherwise, revisions could become a continuing burden on your time.

# OTHER IMPORTANT CLAUSES

Many of the following provisions are frequently omitted from publishers' contracts. Since they are generally helpful, and basically noncontroversial, you should ask that they be included.

**Advertising and Material by Others**
Include a clause that prohibits advertisements and material by others in the book unless you give your written consent. (An exception can be provided for ads for other books by the same publisher.) Require the publisher to put a similar prohibition in any contract it signs to license rights in your book.

**Reservation of Rights**
• Be sure that a clause is included stating that "all rights in the Work not specifically granted in this Agreement to the Publisher are reserved to the Author."

**Affiliates**
Include a clause stating that if the publisher licenses any rights or sells any books to a company affiliated with the publisher, then the terms of that contract must be at least as good as they would have been if the contract was made with a nonaffiliated party. A good definition for "affiliated com-

pany" is "any company controlling, controlled by or under common control with the publisher." An alternative way of providing this is to say the contract can be entered into only after "arms-length" negotiations, i.e., negotiations that are conducted as if the companies were unrelated.

## Arbitration

Ask for a clause that any disputes under the contract be submitted to arbitration. This procedure is generally simpler, quicker and less costly than lawsuits in courts. Some publishers refuse to give this as a matter of policy (generally the larger ones with their own legal staffs); smaller ones are more apt to appreciate the benefits of arbitration.

## Assignment

Prohibit assignment (i.e., a transfer) of the contract by your publisher to another publisher without your consent and say that any such assignment is void. Prudent publishers will want an exception for assignments in connection with the sale of substantially all of the publisher's assets; in general, this is not objectionable.[32]

## Right to Audit

There should be a clause allowing you or a representative to audit the publisher's accounting records to determine the accuracy of your royalty statements. This is rarely objectionable. You should also try to provide that the cost of the audit will be borne by the publisher if the audit shows that the publisher shortchanged you by $x\%$ (often 5%) or more on the statements being audited.

## Credit

If there is more than one author, clarify whose name will come first, whether both names will be the same size and whether the two names will be joined by "and," "with" or some other word.[33]

## Return of Manuscript and Art

The contract will frequently provide that the publisher is not responsible for any loss or damage to the manuscript or any artwork or related material submitted by the author. Ask that the phrase "provided Publisher has exercised reasonable care with respect thereto" or, at the least, "other than in the case of Publisher's gross negligence or willful misconduct" be added to the clause.

Illustrators may also wish to include a clause requiring the publisher to promptly return all original art as soon as the plates or film is made (or as soon as the book is printed, if the illustrations are in color and needed for on-press color checks).

## Free Copies

If you need more than the number stated in the contract, don't be reluctant to ask. It's one of the easiest changes for the publisher to make; the increased cost to the publisher is only the book's incremental manufacturing cost, often no more than $2 a copy. Be sure to specify that the number of free copies applies separately to hardcover and paperback editions if the publisher does both.

Virtually all contracts also contain a provision allowing the author to purchase additional copies at 40% to 50% off the retail price (the same discount offered to booksellers and wholesalers); if for some reason this clause is not in your contract, ask that it be inserted.

## Governing Law

Be sure there is a provision stating which state's laws apply in case of a dispute.

## Paperback

If any special clauses in your contract are meant to apply to paperback or other reprint editions by another publisher, make that clear, either within the clause itself or separately. Examples of these clauses are those about copyright notices, advertising prohibitions and approvals of cover designs.

# APPENDIX

## Sample Letter of Comments

An author's request for changes to the publisher's contract is typically contained in a letter to the person who sent the contract, generally the book's editor or someone in the contracts department.

The sample below will give you an idea of the style, tone and format of a typical letter. *The comments are illustrative only*; you should decide what points you want to include in your letter after carefully reading the publisher's contract, comparing it section by section with the topics discussed in this book, and deciding what is important to you for the book you are writing. Don't forget to consider topics discussed in the book that are omitted entirely from the publisher's contract.

In organizing your letter, it is best to follow the order of the publisher's contract so they can easily follow your comments and make the suggested revisions. Where a comment applies to a particular word or phrase, it is also helpful to indicate the line on which that word or phrase appears.

[Date]

_____, Editor
SVH Publishing Company
[Address]
[City, State, Zip]

Dear _____:

I am delighted that SVH will be publishing my book and that you will be my editor. I have read the contract you sent me last week and have the following comments. I don't think they should give you much trouble but if there are any that do, please let me know and we can discuss them further. For your convenience and that of your contracts department, I have attempted in each heading to identify the section in your contract to which my comment relates.

Section _____ * [grant of rights]

In the [third] line, please replace the phrase "in whole or in part" with "in whole but not in part, and in book form only."

Please provide that if the British Commonwealth rights or the rights for any foreign language are not licensed within three years of the book's initial U.S. publication, then those unlicensed rights will automatically revert to me.**

---

*State the specific section or subsection to which your comment applies, e.g., *Section 3(g)(ii)*. Since I am not referring to a specific contract in my example, I have instead indicated in brackets the topic that the section relates to; the material in brackets need not appear in your letter.

**For those contracts which provide that "all rights" are granted to the publisher, your comment can simply be: "The statement in the [second] line that I am granting you 'all rights' in the work is overly broad. Please list the specific rights that you are seeking."

Section _____ [time for delivery of manuscript]

In line [five], please delete the phrase "time is of the essence."

At the end of the paragraph, please provide that if the manuscript is late, you will not terminate the contract unless you first send me written notice that it is late and give me an additional 30 days to deliver it.

Section _____ [description of manuscript]

In the [third] line, please insert 120,000-140,000 words as the approximate length of the manuscript. At the end of this section, please add a sentence describing the book as "a serious history of Washington, D.C. during 1940-1944, written for a general audience and based on the author's experience as a UPI reporter covering FDR and the War Department, unpublished interviews from the period, current interviews with still-living participants and material obtained under the Freedom of Information Act. The book will be written in the same general style as the two draft chapters submitted to the Publisher in April and will not be extensively footnoted."

In the [sixth] line, please delete the phrase "together with all illustrations, drawings, maps and such other material as Publisher requests." It is my understanding that all I am expected to deliver is the text of my manuscript, 10 black-and-white photographs and three charts. (If this is not the case, please call me so we can discuss exactly what you want me to deliver and change the contract to reflect that.)

In the [eighth] line, please insert "approximately ten 4 × 5 inch black-and-white" before the word "photographs."

Please delete the requirement in the [tenth] line that I deliver the charts to you "in form suitable for reproduction." I will be glad to give you rough sketches of how they should look but you should be getting (and paying for) an artist to put them in whatever shape you need for publication.

In line [12], please delete the index as an item I am to deliver. Instead, provide that you will have the index prepared on a work-for-hire basis by a person satisfactory to both of us, that the index will be submitted to me for my approval and revisions before it is set in type, and that you and I will split the cost of having the index prepared (with you advancing my half of the cost and deducting it from future royalties if and after my advance earns out).

Section _____ [acceptance of manuscript]

In lines [6] and [9], please add "in form and content" after the word "satisfactory" in both places that it appears.

Please state that you will notify me within 30 days after I deliver my manuscript that it is accepted or give me written suggestions for revision if it is not. Also provide that if you do not give me this written notice and I send you a reminder, then the manuscript will be deemed satisfactory and accepted for all purposes of the contract unless I get written suggestions for revisions from you within 21 days after you get my reminder.

Section _____ [changes in manuscript]

At the end of the [second] sentence, please change "spelling, grammar and style" to "spelling and grammar" and add the following as a third sentence: "Other than as stated in the preceding sentence, no change will be made in the manuscript without the Author's approval."

Section _____ [title]

Please provide that there will be no changes in the book's title from that specified in the contract without my consent.

Section _____ [representations and warranties]

At the end of this section, please add "These representations and warranties do not apply to any material furnished by Publisher."

Section _____ [indemnification]

In lines [3] and [7], delete the references to "claims, actions and proceedings." Instead, please provide that I will be required to indemnify you only against final non-appealable judgments based upon a breach of my representations and warranties (and related expenses).

In line [10], please delete "and under any other contracts between Publisher and the Author."

Section _____ [publication]

Please add a section stating that you will publish the book within one year after you accept the manuscript (or it is deemed accepted, as provided above). Please also provide that if you do not and I give you written notice of your failure to do so, then the contract will automatically terminate 60 days after my notice to you unless you have published the book before the end of that 60-day period. The contract should also state that if the contract is so terminated, all rights will automatically revert to me and I will be entitled to keep all advances previously paid and to receive any parts of my advance not yet paid.

Section _____ [copyright]

Please copyright the book in my name, rather than yours. Also, please specifically state that you will print a proper copyright notice in each copy of the book and require each licensee to do the same (to the extent applicable to the medium).

Section _____ [advance]

Please add the following at the end of this section: "Other than as specifically provided in this Agreement, no amounts paid or payable by Publisher in connection with the Work may be deducted from the Author's advance, royalties or any other monies payable to the Author under this Agreement."

Section _____ [reduced royalties]

In [clause (iv)], please provide that the reduced royalty only applies to sales outside ordinary wholesale and retail book channels. Alternatively, please change "50% or more" to "more than 55%" for the hardcover edition and for trade paperbacks. In that case, please also provide that in no event shall the reduced royalty rate ever be less than half the regular rate (except for premium and special sales).*

Please specify that sales of books to which the reduced royalty applies nonetheless count toward the total number of books sold for purposes of determining when the regular royalty rate escalates.

Section _____ [small printings]

In [clause (v)], please state that the provision does not apply to the initial printing nor to any year when total sales for the year are more than 1,000 copies. Also, rather than

_____

*Instead of the last two sentences, you could also say: "Alternatively, please provide that on copies sold at a discount of more than [50%] from the retail price, the royalty provided in [clause (a)] shall decrease by 1/2% for each 1% by which the discount exceeds 50% but in no event shall the royalty equal less than one-half of the then-current royalty under [clause (a)]."

cutting the royalty in half on printings of [2,500]* copies or less, I would appreciate your making it 2/3 of the royalty and on printings of 1,000 or less.

## Section ____ [cheap reprints]

Please clarify that the reduced royalty for "cheap" reprint editions applies only to hardcover reprints by inserting the word "hardcover" after "cheap" in the [second] line. Please also define "cheap" as "(i.e., less than half the price at which the book was initially published)."

## Section ____ [subsidiary rights]

Please eliminate the reference to merchandising and commercial rights. Also eliminate all references that grant you any rights to license my characters.

Please eliminate the phrase "electronic, mechanical and other rights, including" and simply keep the list of specified rights that is there.

Please state that you will promptly notify me of any rights licensed and give me copies of the licensing agreements.

## Section ____ [division of proceeds]

In [clause (iii)], please provide that all amounts above [$100,000] earned from licensing mass market paperback rights will be split 60% for me and 40% for the publisher.

In [clause (vii)], please change "75%" to "80%" (British rights).

---

*Numbers or amounts in brackets are hypothetical ones solely for purpose of illustration; the number you choose should relate to your particular contract.

At the end of [clause (x)], provide that your right to license performance, movie, audio and computer rights will revert to me at the end of three years from the book's initial publication to the extent not licensed by that time. Also provide that contracts licensing any of these rights require my prior written approval.

Please provide that if you retain an agent to license any of these subsidiary rights, the amounts paid to the agent will be deducted only from your share of the proceeds.

Please provide somewhere in this section that if my share of any subsidiary rights payments is more than [$1,000] after my advance has earned out, then you will pay me my share of the proceeds within 30 days after you get it.

Section _____ [royalty statements]

Please change "four months" to "three months" in line 3 and provide that royalties will be paid twice a year, not once a year.

Please provide that even if royalties are less than [$25] in any period you will still provide me with a royalty statement.

In the [sixth] line, please insert "reasonable" before "reserve for returns." Please also provide that, with each royalty statement, you will notify me of the amount being withheld as a reserve against returns. In addition, please add a clause saying that you will not hold any reserves for returns on books shipped more than three accounting periods prior to the date of the latest royalty statement.

Section _____ [out of print]

Please define "out of print" as follows: "The Work shall be considered 'in print' only when copies of an English-language book edition of the Work are regularly available and offered for sale in the United States by the Publisher or its licensee in sufficient quantities for general distribution to bookstores and the book is included in the Publisher's or such licensee's most recent catalog."

Section ____ [option]

Please provide that I shall only be required to deliver an outline and a sample chapter, not a full manuscript.

Provide that the option begins from the time my manuscript for this book is accepted, not from when the book is published.

In line [eight], change two months to four weeks, and provide that if I don't hear from you during that time, you will be considered to have waived your option rights.

Delete "financial" before "terms" in the [fourth] line from the bottom. Also eliminate the last sentence ("If another . . . upon the same terms and conditions"). If another publisher has spent the time and effort and made an offer on the book after you have turned it down, it's not fair for you to be able to match their offer.

Section ____ [competitive works]

Please provide that this section will apply only for two years after the book's initial publication. Also provide that it will not prevent me from doing other books that are expansions of one or two of the chapters in the book. Please also make it clear that it applies only to books and does not prevent me from writing magazine articles or articles for professional journals. Provide too that this section does not apply to any textbook that I might decide to write on the same subject or to any kind of book I write on the same subject for teenagers or younger children.

Section _____ [next book]

Saying that this will be the next book I publish seems onerous, especially since you will control timing of publication. Either delete this section entirely or change it to provide that I will not enter into any contract with a publisher that requires me to deliver a manuscript to them before I deliver my manuscript for this book to you.

Section _____ [revised editions]

Please delete the entire section and say instead that the book will not be revised unless we both agree. I think that is the simplest way to handle things. If this is not acceptable, however, then please provide the following in this section:

1. If you decide to revise the book, I will have the right to do it myself or to get someone to do it under my supervision.

2. If you get someone else to do the revision, limit the amount of money paid to that person which can be deducted from my royalties and subsidiary rights payments to 50% of what I would otherwise be entitled to if the edition is the first I haven't worked on, 75% if it's the second I haven't worked on and 90% if it's the third or one subsequent to the third. Also provide that any work done by that person will be on a work for hire basis for copyright purposes.

3. Provide that if that person is to be given coauthorship credit, my name will be listed first, as the main author. Further provide that, if I am alive, any revision done by someone you hire will be delivered to me for my approval. Also state that if I don't approve of the revision, you will remove my name as author of the book.

*Other Clauses*

Please add the following clauses at the end of your contract:

*Advertising.* Advertising (other than of other books published by the publisher of the edition in question), or material by others, may not be inserted or printed in any edition of the Work, whether issued by Publisher or its licensee, without the Author's written consent.

*Reservation of Rights.* All rights in the Work not specifically granted in this Agreement to Publisher are reserved to the Author.

*Abridgments.* The Author shall have the right to approve any abridgment, condensation or adaptation of the Work which Publisher is authorized to license pursuant to this Agreement.

*Audit.* Upon written request and at a mutually convenient time during ordinary business hours, the Author or a representative may examine Publisher's books and records relating to the Work at Publisher's office. Any such examination shall be at the Author's expense unless accounting errors amounting to more than 5% of the sum paid to the Author pursuant to this Agreement for the accounting periods being reviewed are found to the Author's disadvantage.

*Affiliates.* Except as otherwise provided in this Agreement, any license granted, or copies of the Work sold, by Publisher under this Agreement to a person or entity related to or affiliated with the Publisher shall be granted or sold on financial and other terms which are no less favorable to Publisher than the terms upon which Publisher would have granted such license, or sold such copies, to an unrelated or unaffiliated person or entity.

*Arbitration.* Any controversy or claim arising out of or relating to this Agreement, or the breach thereof, shall be settled by arbitration in accordance with the commercial arbitration rules of the American Arbitration Association, and judgment upon the award rendered by the arbitrators may be entered in any court having jurisdiction thereof.

I look forward to hearing from you. Please feel free to give me a call if you have a problem with any of these so I can explain my concern and we can work something out that is satisfactory to both of us.

Thank you.

Very truly yours,

Lisa S. Michael

# NOTES

1  Objections to such a broad grant of rights are numerous: the publisher should know what it needs and can sell; rights should not be granted unwittingly; the publisher may not be the best person to exploit these rights; if you are granting all rights, you should be receiving fair compensation for each in advance; doing so may prevent the author from writing further books involving the work and characters he or she has created.

2  These countries are the principal members of what is still referred to as the British Commonwealth of Nations. The countries outside the United States, the British Commonwealth and Canada are called the "Open Market."

3  Although an author rightly grants all these rights to publishers, small press publishers licensing reprint rights and book producers might not always find it beneficial to do so.

4  Small press publishers selling reprint rights to paperback houses, however, typically license a work only for a specified period of time, generally between five and ten years. Other matters of concern to small presses licensing reprint rights to mass market publishers are discussed in my article, "Negotiating Reprint Rights with the Majors," which appeared in the March 1986 issue of *Small Press* magazine.

5  The longer period of time, 90 days, is appropriate for books on specialized subjects where the publisher has to send the manuscript to outside experts for review before deciding whether to accept and publish it. For books where the editor, alone or with

others in the house, is making the final judgment, 60 days should be sufficient.

6 A cautious author would negotiate these provisions anyway and provide that they will apply if the publisher's insurance policy is not in effect when the book is published or if the insurance company's liability under the policy has already been used up by other lawsuits against the publisher.

7 For further information about "work for hire," see "Whose Copyright Is It Anyway?" originally published in *Small Press* (January 1985). The law in this area is susceptible to change, however, and you should ascertain that the information in that article is still current before relying on it. See also Note 13.

The Authors Guild is located at 234 West 44th Street, New York, New York 10036. The New York office of VLA is located at 1285 Avenue of the Americas, New York, New York 10019; there are also VLA chapters in Chicago, Washington, D.C., Philadelphia, Houston, Denver, San Francisco and other cities.

8 See pages 11–13.

9 E.g., deductions for author's failure to provide the index or other illustrations if author is required to do so and publisher has to do it instead; deductions for copies of the book purchased by author from publisher.

10 I.e., if the manuscript is not delivered on time or if it is not satisfactory.

11 Some publishers simply insert "nonreturnable" before advance. From the author's viewpoint, this is fine although the quoted language is more accurate.

12 The following table shows equivalences between royalties based on list and those based on net for discounts of 20%, 40% and 50%. If the average

| discount is: | 20% | 40% | 50% |
|---|---|---|---|
| then: | | | |
| 10% of list equals | 12 1/2% of net | 16 2/3% net | 20% net |
| 12.5% of list equals | 15 5/8% of net | 20.8 % net | 25% net |
| 15% of list equals | 18 3/4% of net | 25 % net | 30% net |

[13] Note that royalties can be paid in a work for hire arrangement, even though they generally are not. "Work for hire" is a concept that governs who owns the copyright to a work, not the manner in which the person doing the work is paid. Also see the discussion about "work for hire" on page 22.

[14] As distinguished from mass market paperbacks. Although there is no standard industry definition for the difference, mass market paperbacks are generally the pocket-sized, lower priced ones which are heavily distributed in newsstands and supermarkets as well as bookstores and which are returned to the publisher by ripping off the cover and returning only the cover. Trade paperbacks are generally more expensive than the mass market paperback and are frequently the same size as the hardcover; they are typically sold through the same distribution channels as hardcover books and returned in the same way that hardcovers are.

[15] In that case, the publisher has nothing to lose because it doesn't expect to sell that many copies anyway. And you get the benefit of the higher rate if, as you believe and hope, the book sells better than the publisher's expectations.

[16] An alternative way would be for the publisher to guarantee that your total royalties for any period will never be less than 80% of what the amount would be if royalties were based on list, at least for sales to individuals, schools, bookstores, libraries, wholesalers and distributors (and with the exception of "remainders").

[17] Certain of these deductions *might* be valid in certain premium sales but, if so, that should be clarified in the definition of net in that section, and the author's percentage adjusted upward accordingly.

[18] Not all publishers who use the phrase intend for it to be construed this way. Those using it innocently will be glad to clarify the issue. For those who understand and mean what they are saying, the recommended change is all the more important.

[19] Several major wholesalers now buy books from publishers at 50% off the suggested retail price, rather than the more traditional 46-48% for hardcover books. This new figure is often the same or greater than the discount specified in the contract (typically 48 or 50%) that triggers sharply reduced royalties. This is particularly

significant because, with the exception of initial sales before publication, bookstores order most of their books from wholesalers. Thus, if an author's royalties are reduced on sales to wholesalers at 50% or more, most of the royalties paid to authors for books sold through bookstores—sales on which authors have traditionally received full royalties—are instead paid at a drastically reduced rate.

[20] On sales above 60%, the publisher's traditional formula for reducing royalties is generally okay since at that point one is dealing with premiums and other special sales. See page 36.

[21] The reason for 44% is apparently historical. It presumably represents what the publisher considers the average discount it grants on all the books its sells through traditional channels.

[22] The language for this might be:

> "Where the discount on copies of the trade hardcover or trade paperback editions sold through ordinary book trade channels in the United States is 50% or greater (but less than 60%), the applicable royalty rate provided in section ____ above shall be reduced by one-half the difference between 44% and the discount granted, but in no event shall it be less than one-half the rate otherwise provided in section ____."

[23] Some authors' organizations suggest that any deep discount provisions should apply only when the increased discount is given because a bookstore or wholesaler is ordering a large number of copies of just your book and not simply getting a discount because it is ordering a large number of assorted titles. Although a helpful provision for authors to get, it is frequently resisted by publishers because it is good business for publishers (and helpful to authors) to offer higher discounts to stores ordering large quantities, whether of the same or different titles. Accordingly, I have not listed it as a clause that the typical author should strive for.

[24] In situations such as premiums, royalties can be based on the amount received by the publisher or they can be a percentage, most appropriately one-half, of the amount the publisher is paid in excess of its manufacturing costs for the books and any commissions it had to pay for the sale.

²⁵ Other than Canada.

²⁶ E.g., merchandising rights should not terminate only when the book contract does (i.e., when the book is "out of print"). Merchandising rights are licensed for relatively brief time periods (e.g., three years) and subject to renewal only if the licensed products have been actually produced and sold.

The contract should also make clear that "commercial rights," if granted, do not authorize the publisher to license the author's name as endorsing any product.

²⁷ For example, "Notwithstanding anything to the contrary contained in this Agreement, nothing contained in this Agreement shall be construed to grant to the Publisher any right in the characters, situations or places contained in the Work."

²⁸ I.e., when the total amount of royalties and subsidiary rights income already earned by the book equals or is greater than the author's advance. In inserting a clause like this in a contract, be sure to specify that amounts earned but not yet paid for the current or a previous royalty period are added to royalties already paid in determining whether the advance has earned out.

²⁹ Although this minimum is sometimes only $25 or $10, without the recommended provision you won't know if the publisher forgot to send you a statement, if the statement got lost in the mail or if royalties on the book were simply below the minimum.

³⁰ The effectiveness of this clause will depend on the bankruptcy court supervising the publisher's business. Generally speaking, once a petition for bankruptcy is filed by a publisher, the bankruptcy court must approve a contract's termination for the termination to be valid; in addition, any termination that occurred 90 days before the bankruptcy filing can also be nullified.

³¹ For a discussion of problems frequently encountered between collaborators and the need for collaboration agreements before coauthors get too far along on a project, see my article, "Double Trouble," in the March 1985 issue of *Writer's Digest* (pages 34-35) and reprinted in the Winter 1988 issue of the *Authors Guild Bulletin* (pages 32–33).

[32] Some publishers will also ask for an exception permitting them to assign the contract to a subsidiary of the publisher or to a parent or sister company. If you would not want to be published by one of these other companies, then you should not agree to such an exception; otherwise it is not offensive.

[33] See Note 31.

## About the Author

Mark L. Levine is a lawyer with the New York office of Sullivan & Worcester. His articles about publishing have appeared in *Writers Digest*, the *Authors Guild Bulletin* and *Small Press* magazine. He regularly conducts seminars about book publishing contracts for authors, editors and publishers.

This is Levine's third book. He is co-editor of *The Tales of Hoffman* (Bantam Books 1970), a documentary of courtroom confrontations from the "Chicago 7" Conspiracy Trial, and *The Complete Book of Bible Quotations* (Pocket Books 1986). He is also founder and publisher of Scarf Press, a two-book publishing company, and a former vice president and member of the Board of Directors of the American Book Producers Association.

Levine is a graduate of Columbia College, the Columbia University Graduate School of Journalism and New York University School of Law (where he was a member of the Law Review). A native of Bath, Maine, he has been a lawyer since 1969.

He is a member of The Authors Guild.

# INDEX

Abridgments, 39, 45, 77

Acceptance of manuscript, 11–13, 25, 70. *See also* Satisfactory manuscript

Adaptations, 22, 45, 77

Additions to manuscript, 15, 20, 63

Advance, 5, 20, 23–27, 44
  amount payable on acceptance, 13
  amount payable on publication, 52
  deductions from, 10, 26
  return of, 11–12, 15
  revised editions, 60, 62

Advertising, 63, 66, 77

Affiliated companies, 42, 63–64, 77

Agented rights, 4–5, 23, 26, 41, 43–44
  list of, 40

Agents, 4–5, 24, 41

"Amount received", 28, 33, 34, 82 (n. 24). *See also* Net royalties

Animation. *See* Performance rights

Anthologies, 39

Arbitration, 64, 78

Arms-length, 61, 63–64, 77

Artwork. *See* Illustrations

Assignment of contract, 64

Assorted titles, 82 (n. 23)

Audio rights, 40, 41, 43

Audit, right to, 64, 77

Australia. *See* Commonwealth rights

Authority to sign, 14–15, 59

Authors Guild, 22, 80 (n. 7)

Authorship credit, 61–62, 64

Bad debt, 33, 48

Bankruptcy, 49

Bonuses, 25

Book clubs, 5, 39, 44

Book jackets. *See* Cover

Book producers, 19, 79 (n. 3)

Breach by author, 7, 11, 14–16, 27, 52

Breach by publisher, 20, 49

Breach of representations, 16–18, 25, 27, 52

Break points. *See* Escalating royalties

British Commonwealth. *See* Commonwealth rights

British rights. *See* Commonwealth rights

Cable. *See* Performance rights

Calendars, 46
Camera ready, 8
Canada, 4, 40
Cancellation of contract. *See* Termination
Cartoons, 46
Cassettes. *See* Recording rights
Changes in manuscript, 12–13, 15, 20, 63, 70
Characters, 3, 42, 58
Charts, 7–10
Cheap editions, 38, 73
Children's books, 2, 8–9, 30, 43
Claims. *See* Indemnification
Collaborations, 15, 56, 64–65, 83 (n. 31)
Color separations, 8–9
Comic strips, 46
Commercial rights. *See* Merchandising
Commonwealth rights, 4–5, 40–41, 43, 68, 79 (n. 2)
Competitive books, 14, 57–58, 75
Computer rights, 40–41, 43
Condensations, 39, 45, 77
Consultation rights, 21
Copyright, 9, 21, 22, 61, 71. *See also* Permissions; Work for hire
Copyright notice, 21, 66, 71
Cover, 9, 21, 61
Credit as author, 61–62, 64–65

Credit risk, 33, 48
Cross-collateralization, 19

Damage to manuscript, 65
Deductions from royalties, 10, 18, 19, 26, 33, 60–61
"Deep discount" royalties, 33–37, 72, 82 (n. 20)
Delivery of manuscript, 7–9, 12, 52
Description of manuscript, 7–9
Discounts, 28, 31, 34, 65, 80 (n. 12). *See also* "Deep discount" royalties
Dramatic rights. *See* Performance rights

"Earned out", 44, 83 (n. 28)
Editor's comments, 12–13
Electronic rights, 41
Employee, 15, 22. *See also* Work for hire
Endorsements, 83 (n. 26)
England. *See* Commonwealth rights
English-language rights, 4, 15, 23, 40, 41, 43.
Escalating royalties, 29–31, 36–37, 72
Excerpts, 39. *See also* Serial rights
Exclusivity, 4
Expenses, 8–10, 16, 26, 31, 33

Failure to deliver manuscript, 7, 52
Failure to publish, 20, 25, 49
Film, 52–53
First proceeds, 11–12
First refusal, right of. *See* Option
First serial. *See* Serial rights
Flow-through, 26, 44–45, 74
Foreign rights, 4–5. *See also* Agented rights; Translations; World rights
Free copies, 65

Geographical area, 4–5, 15, 42, 57–58
Good faith, 12, 55
Governing law, 65
Grammar, 20, 70
Grant of rights, 3–6, 23, 41, 68. *See also* Subsidiary rights; Work for hire

Hard/soft deals, 29, 42
Hardcover, 4, 23, 29–30, 35, 38, 46

Illustrations, 2, 7–10, 20, 22, 30, 65
Illustrators, 2. *See also* Illustrations
In print. *See* Out of print
Indemnification, 16–17, 71
Index, 7–10, 13, 70, 80 (n. 9)
Insurance, 16
Interest, 18

Ireland. *See* Commonwealth rights

Judgments, 17, 71

Language of rights, 3–4, 15, 57–58. *See also* Agented rights; Translations
Large print, 5
Lateness, 7, 20, 69
Law governing, 65
Lawsuits, 15–18, 71
Lawyers, 1, 15, 17, 24, 42
Letter of comments, 2, 67–78
Libel, 15. *See also* Indeminification
Licensing agent, 44
Licensing rights. *See* Grant of rights; Subsidiary rights
List, 28–34
Loss of manuscript, 65

Mail order, 38
Manufacturing costs, 32, 82 (n. 24)
Manuscript, 7–13
  acceptance of, 11–13, 70
  additions by others, 63
  changes in, 12–13, 15, 20
  damage to, 65
  delivery of, 7–9, 12
  description of, 7–9
  editor's response, 12–13
  lateness, 7, 69

return of, 65
satisfactory, 8, 11–13, 25, 52
specificity required, 7–9
time of delivery, 7
Maps, 8
Material by others, 63
Mechanical rights, 41
Merchandising, 3, 41–42, 44
Movie rights. *See* Performing rights

Net income, 32–33
Net proceeds, 32, 42
Net (royalties), 28–29, 31–33, 36, 82 (n. 24). *See also* Amount received
New Zealand. *See* Commonwealth rights
"Next book" clause, 14, 59, 76. *See also* Option
Noncompetition. *See* Competitive books

Obligation to publish, 15, 20, 71
Obscenity, 15
"Open market", 79 (n. 2)
Option, 14, 54–56, 58, 75
Other contracts, relationship with, 19
Out of print, 6, 14, 50–51, 74

Paperbacks. *See also* Reprint rights
general, 4, 42–44, 66

mass and trade distinguished, 81 (n. 14)
royalties, 29–30, 35
Pass-through. *See* Flow-through
Performance rights, 3, 5, 40, 42–43, 45. *See also* Agented rights
Permissions, 9–10, 15
Philippines, 4
Photographs, 8–10. *See also* Illustrations
Plates, 52–53
Plays. *See* Performance rights
Premiums, 5, 36, 39, 81 (n. 17), 82 (n. 20), 82 (n. 24)
Print, out of. *See* Out of print
Privacy, 15
Pseudonyms, 56
Publish, failure to, 20, 25, 49
Publish, obligation to, 20, 71
Puerto Rico, 4

Quotations, 39

Readings, 39
Receipts, 33
Recording rights, 39–41, 43, 45–46
Reduced royalties, 33–38, 72, 82 (n. 20), 82 (n. 23)
Rejection of manuscript. *See* Satisfactory manuscript
Remainders, 53, 81 (n. 16)
Repayments to publisher, 10,

11–12, 15, 26–27. *See
also* Indemnification
epresentations, 14–15, 71
breach of, 16–18, 25, 27, 52
eprint rights, 4, 39, 42, 43–
44, 46, 66, 79 (n. 4)
eprints, low price, 38
eservation of rights, 63
eserve for returns, 48, 74
etail price. *See* List
eturn of manuscript, 65
eturns, 48, 74
eversion of rights, 5, 41,
52, 61, 68, 74. *See also*
Out of print; Termina-
tion of contract
evised editions, 60–62, 76
evisions of manuscript. *See*
Changes in manuscript
ights, grant of. *See* Grant
of rights
ights, reservation of,
ights, reversion of. *See* Reversion of rights
ights retained by agent.
*See* Agented rights
oyalties, 28–38, 50–51
after termination, 52
amount of, 29–32
deductions from, 10, 18,
19, 26, 33, 60–61
deep discount, 33–37, 72
escalations, 29–31, 36–37,
72
list, 28–29, 80 (n. 12)
mail order, 38

maximum amount, 48
net, 28–29, 31–33, 36, 81
(n. 17)
net and list compared, 28,
31, 80 (n. 12)
paperbacks, 29–30
reductions in, 33–38, 72
revised editions, 60–61
small printings, 37–38, 72
typical rates, 29–32
withholding, 17–18
work for hire, 29, 81 (n. 13)
Royalty statements, 47–48,
64, 74

Satisfactory manuscript, 8,
11–13, 25, 52
Second serial. *See* Serial
rights
Sequels, 3, 42, 58
Serial rights, 5, 39–40, 43,
46. *See also* Agented
rights
Series, 3, 42, 58
Settlement, 17
Shipping charges, 33
Short discount, 28, 31, 32
Small printings, 36–38, 72
Softcover. *See* Paperbacks
South Africa. *See* Common-
wealth rights
Special sales. *See* Premiums
Specificity, 3, 6, 7–9, 28–29,
41–42, 50, 57, 79 (n. 1)
Splits, 43–44

Stage rights. *See* Performing rights

Style, 9, 20

Subsidiary rights, 6, 39–46, 63–64, 66, 73–74
  abridgments, 39, 45
  anthologies, 39
  author's share, 43–44
  book club, 5, 39, 44
  computer rights, 40–41, 43
  condensations, 39, 45
  definition of, 39
  excerpts, 39
  flow-through, 26, 44–45, 74
  granted to publisher, 39–40
  income from, 26, 33, 43–45, 73–74
  list of, 39–40
  publisher's share, 43–44
  readings, 39
  recordings, 39–40
  retained by author, 40
  reversion, 41
  serialization, 5, 39–40, 43, 46
  territories, 42
  translations, 5, 15, 23, 40, 41, 43. *See also* Commonwealth rights; Merchandising; Performance rights; Premiums; Reprint rights

Television. *See* Performance rights

Term of contract, 6

Termination of contract, 7, 20, 25, 49–53, 69

Territory of grant, 3–5, 42

Textbooks, 1–65

"Time is of the essence," 7, 69

Time of delivery, 7

Time period of grant, 4, 50–51

Time to publish, 20

Title, ownership of, 45

Title of work, 20–21, 70

Trade books (defined), 28

Trade channels, 34–35

Trade paperbacks, 81 (n. 14). *See also* Paperbacks

Trademarks, 3, 45

Translations, 5, 15, 23, 40, 41, 43, 68. *See also* Agented rights

Typesetting, 31, 53

United States rights, 4, 23

Videocassettes, 40–41, 43, 46

Volunteer Lawyers for the Arts, 22, 80 (n. 7)

Warranties. *See* Representations

"Whole or in part," 5, 68

Wholesalers. *See* Discounts

Work for hire, 3, 22, 29, 61, 81 (n. 13)

World rights, 15, 23, 41